Hi MoM! Hi DaD!

101 cartoons for
New Parents
by Lynn Johnston

Meadowbrook
Distributed by Simon & Schuster
New York

Meadowbrook Press Edition
87   20   19   18

PRINTED IN THE UNITED STATES OF AMERICA
Library of Congress Number 77-82216
ISBN 0-915658-06-2

Published by Meadowbrook, Inc., Deephaven,
MN 55391

BOOK TRADE DISTRIBUTION by Simon and
Schuster, a division of Simon & Schuster, Inc.,
1230 Avenue of the Americas, New York,
NY 10020
S & S Ordering #: 0-671-54482-9

THE FIRST YEAR OF LIFE

A tiny bundle of life is placed in your arms, and at first it's hard to believe that you are now a parent. The overwhelming feeling of responsibility for another life, the pride and joy in your "creation", but also the concomitant feelings of inadequacy in your new role, frequently surface during that first year.

Lynn Johnston, with humour and sensitivity, creates cartoons that depict the feelings and reactions of parents as they learn to respond to the needs of the growing child, to the reactions of in-laws and relatives, to the pressures of the mass media, the experts, and the child-rearing fads. As we chuckle at the captions, we are reminded of the incredible amount of hardship experienced by parents during the baby's first year—the loss of sleep, the feeling of helplessness when the baby cries and can't be comforted, and the new precautions we have to take as the baby acquires new competencies and skills, as he or she learns to reach and grasp objects, sit up, creep, and finally becomes upright and mobile.

The baby becomes a "real" personality and enriches the life of the family. The joy experienced by the parents makes the struggle well worthwhile. The recognition of this joy is captured in the last cartoon: "To think that before we had a baby, this was just the same old park!"

With a few deft strokes of her pen, Lynn Johnston shows us what the first year of life is like. Her delightfully subtle cartoons at once make the hardships of life with baby more bearable.

— *Mary Blum, Psychologist*

Why is it that after nine months, 14 hours labor, an episiotomy and hemorrhoids... I still find it hard to believe you're really here!
LYNN

11

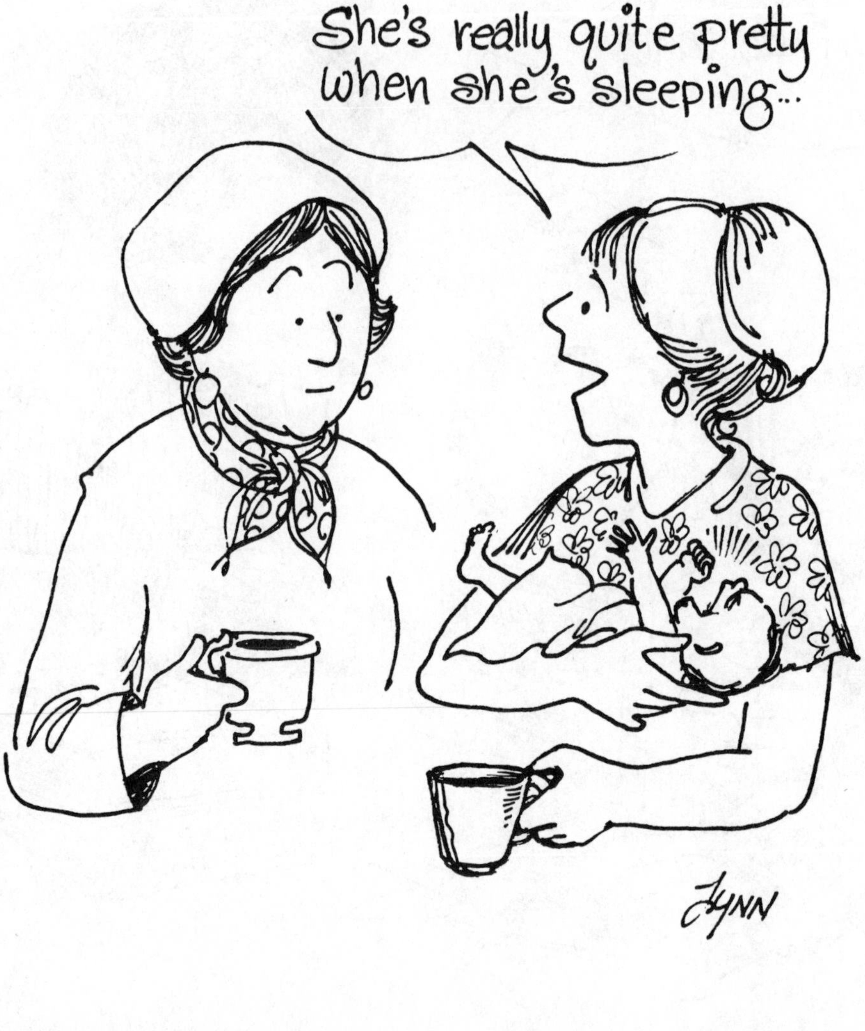
She's really quite pretty when she's sleeping...
LYNN

13

14

15

19

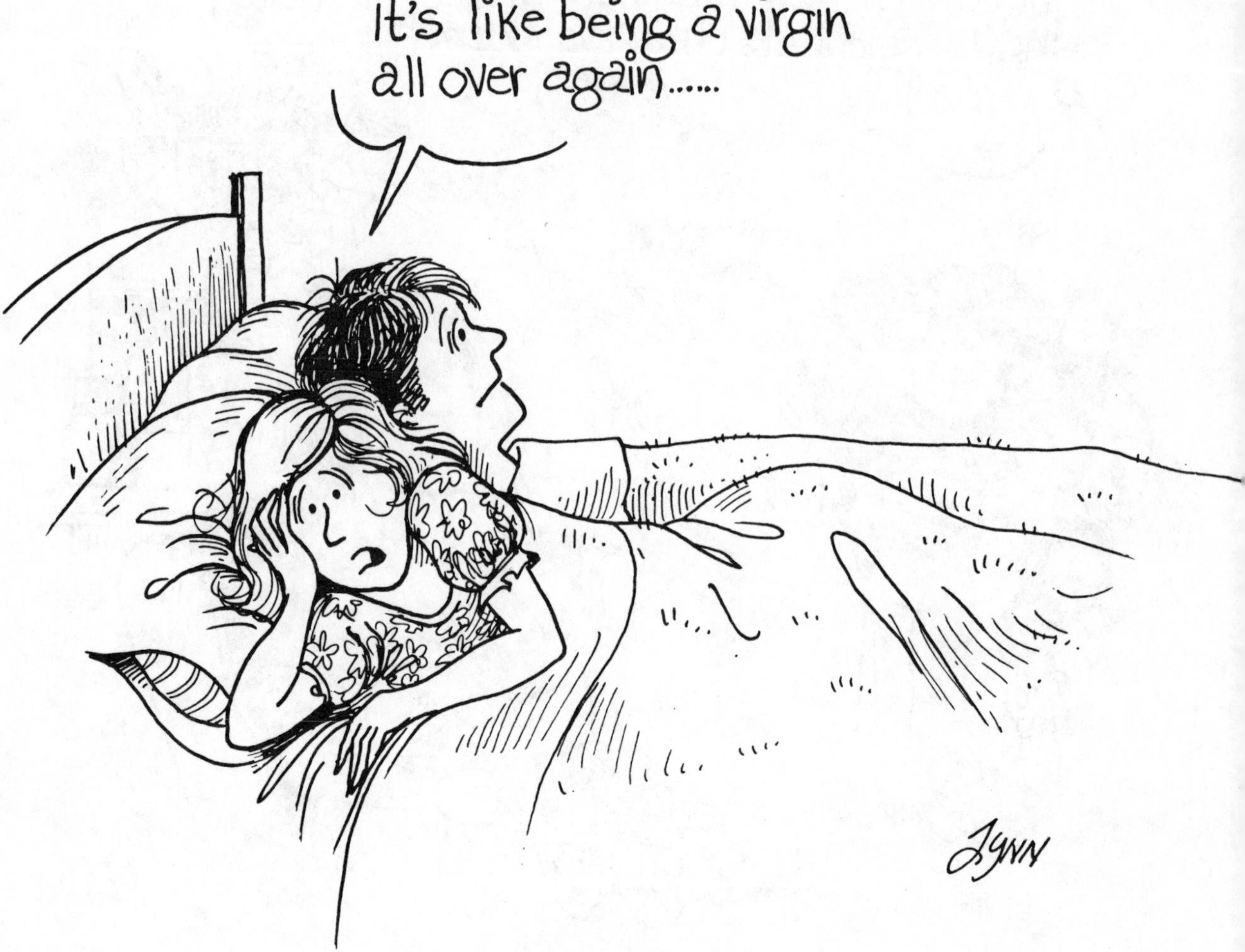
It's like being a virgin all over again......
LYNN

24

Now, Carol, you relax & I'll look after the baby....

25

26

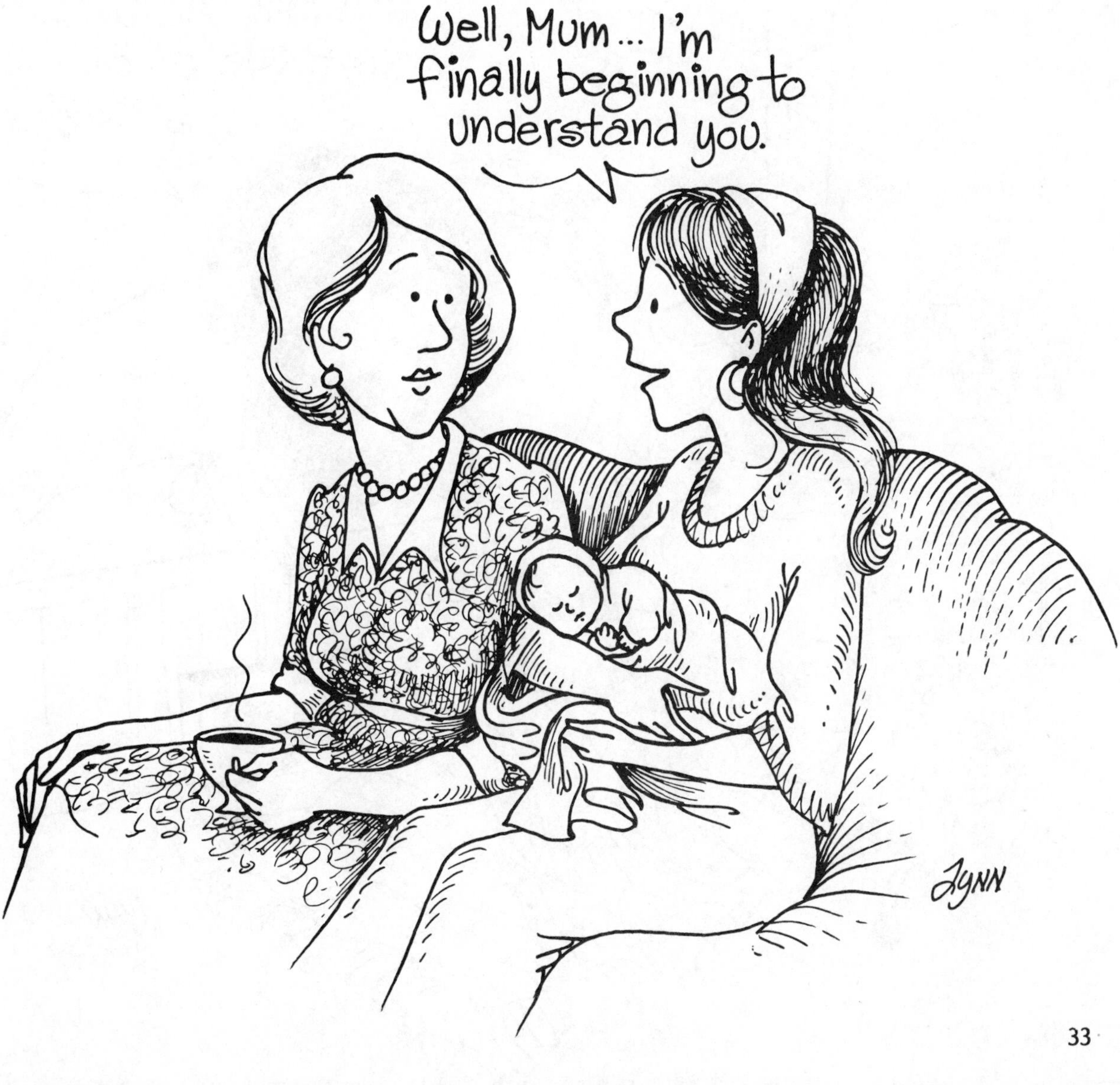
Well, Mum... I'm finally beginning to understand you.
LYNN

34

half the battle is not letting _them_ know that you don't know what the heck you're doing!

I've tried feeding and rocking...and singing...and burping and bathing and pleading...and walking and shouting and whispering and... changing...and....

Dear Mom, you ask if we enjoy parenthood. Well, after 3 weeks of getting used to the situation, I can safely say ~~that we are already~~ that ~~things are~~ ~~that the baby is~~ Mom, can you make it out here?

Lynn

39

41

43

45

48

49

53

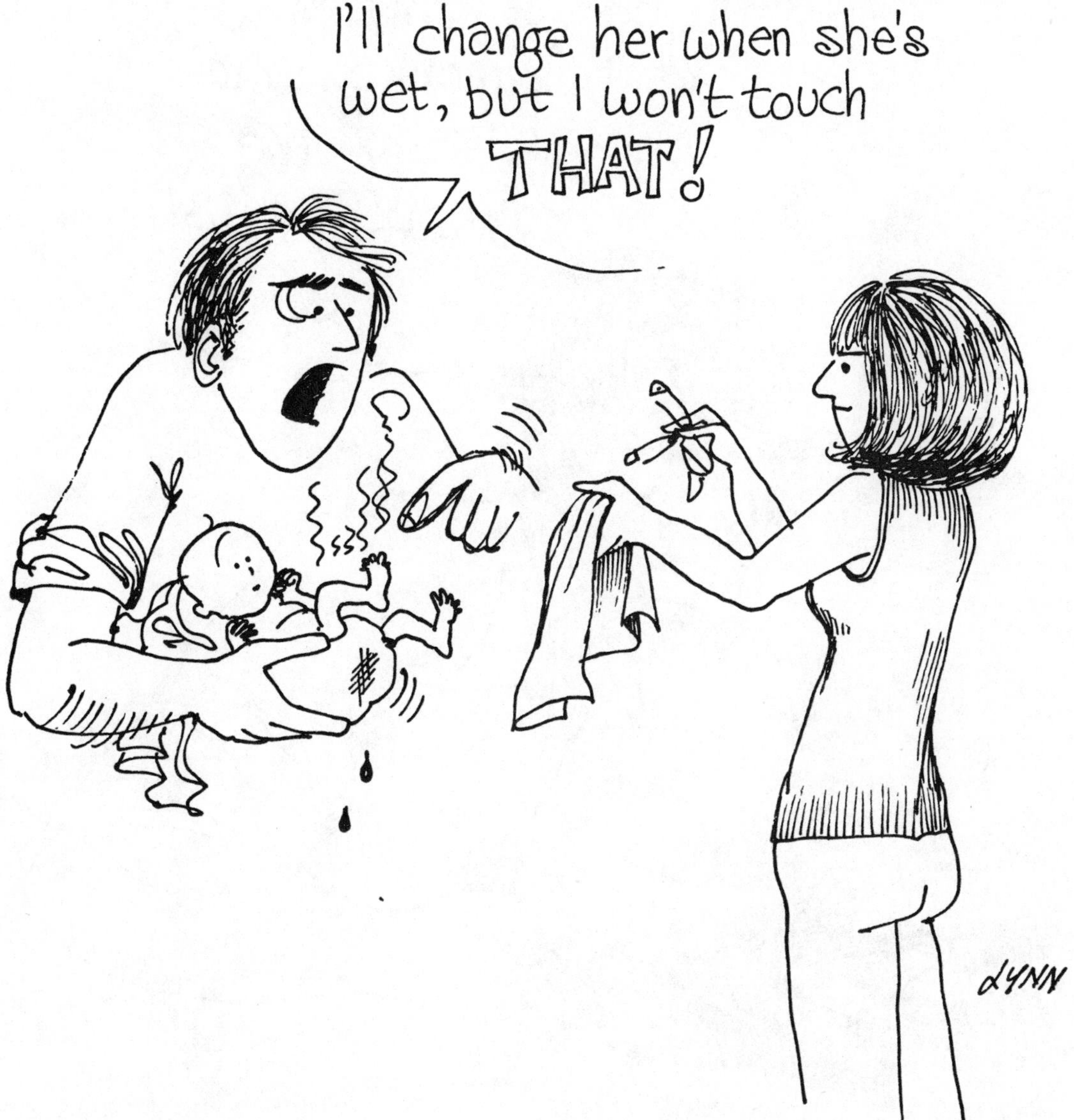
I'll change her when she's wet, but I won't touch THAT!
LYNN

58

66

68

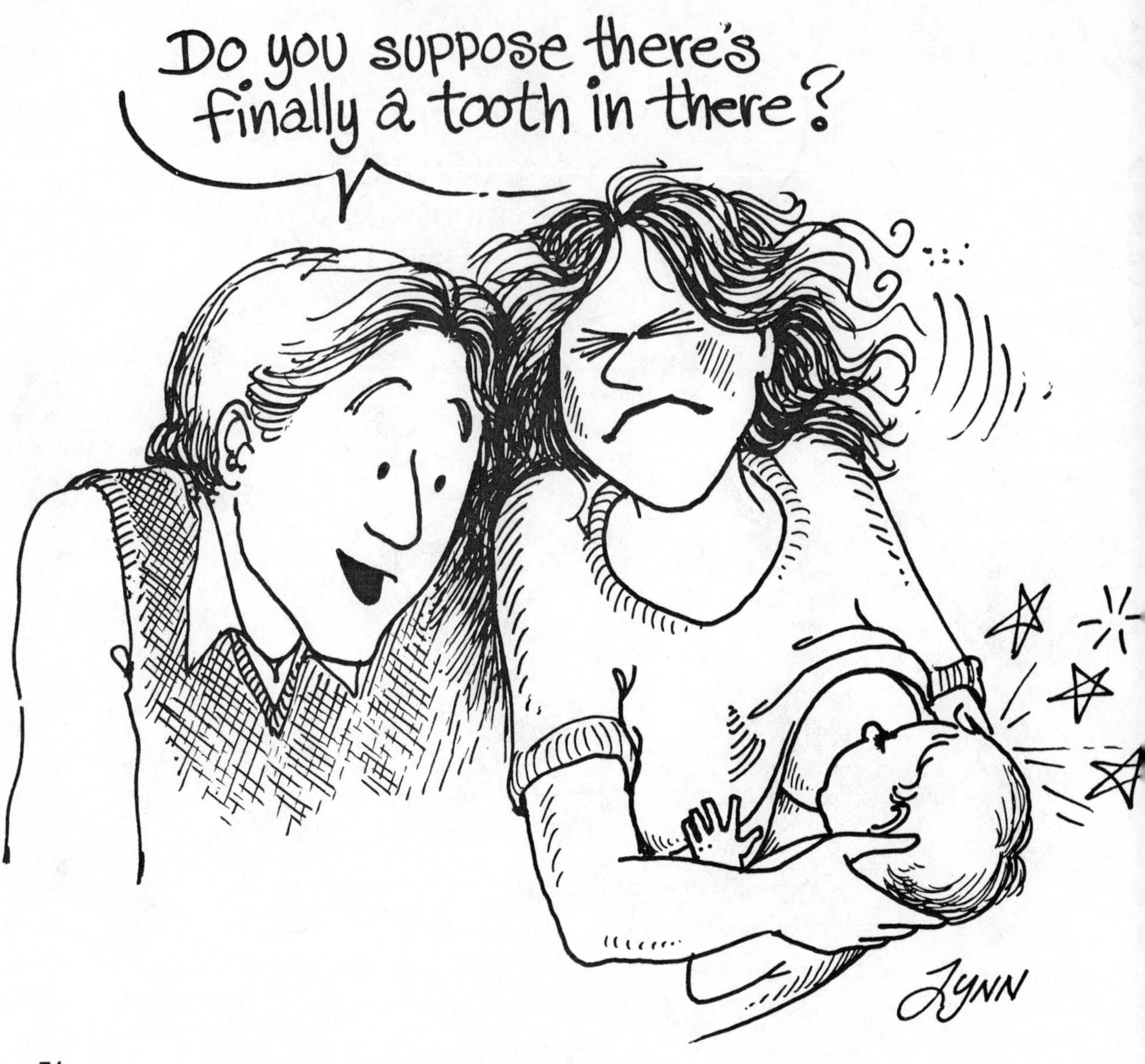
Do you suppose there's finally a tooth in there?
LYNN

Shiela? you were right! threw out all the teething biscuits ..... This could be a new era for MILK BONE!
?
LYNN

Wow! if finding his fingers makes him THIS happy—wait'll he discovers ORIFICES!!

Lynn

78

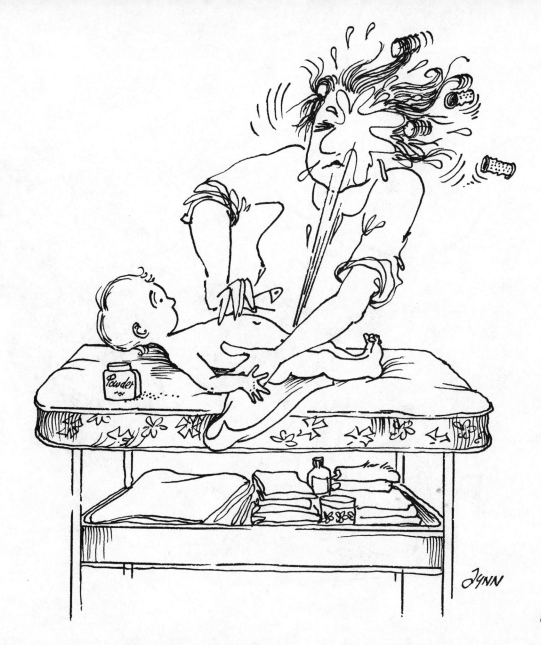

85

94

101

Meet Lynn Johnston

Lynn Johnston is North America's best-selling female cartoonist. She draws much of her material from close observation of her family: Aaron, Katie and husband Rod (a dentist). Lynn's deft, humorous depictions of life with kids have provided her with material for three books published by Meadowbrook, plus an internationally syndicated comic strip, "For Better Or For Worse." Lynn and her family live in Corbeil, Ontario.

& Her Books:

DAVID WE'RE PREGNANT!!
101 laughing out loud cartoons that accentuate the humorous side of conceiving, expecting and giving birth. A great baby shower gift, it's the perfect way to bolster the spirits of any expectant couple.

(S & S Ordering #: 54476-4) $3.95

HI MOM! HI DAD!
A side splitting sequel to DAVID WE'RE PREGNANT! 101 cartoons on the first year of childrearing . . . . . . all those late night wakings, early morning wakings, and other traumatic "emergencies" too numerous to list.

(S & S Ordering #: 54482-9) $3.95

DO THEY EVER GROW UP?
This third in her series of cartoon books is a hilarious survival guide for parents of the tantrum and pacifier set, as well as a side splitting memory book for parents who have lived through it.

(S & S Ordering #: 54478-0) $3.95

Parenting Books

Our Baby's First Year

A Baby Record Calendar
A nursery calendar with 13 undated months for recording "big events" of baby's first year. Each month features animal characters, and baby care and development tips. Photo album page and family tree, too! A great shower gift!

(S & S Ordering #: 54486-1) $7.95

Parents' Guide to Baby & Child Medical Care

by Terril H. Hart, M.D.

A first aid and home treatment guide that shows parents how to handle over 150 common childhood illnesses in a step-by-step illustrated format. Includes a symptoms index, health record forms, child-proofing tips, and more.

(S & S Ordering #: 54470-5) $7.95

Dear Babysitter

With Sitter's Handbook and Instruction Pad

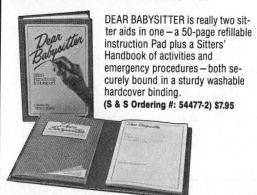

DEAR BABYSITTER is really two sitter aids in one – a 50-page refillable instruction Pad plus a Sitters' Handbook of activities and emergency procedures – both securely bound in a sturdy washable hardcover binding.

(S & S Ordering #: 54477-2) $7.95

Mother Murphy's Law

by Bruce Lansky

The wit of Bombeck and the wisdom of Murphy are combined in this collection of 325 laws that detail the perils and pitfalls of parenthood. Cartoon illustrations by Christine Tripp.

(S&S Ordering #: 62274-9) $2.95

ORDER FORM

Qty.	Order #	Book Title	Author	Price
____	54470-5	Baby and Child Medical Care	Hart, T.	$ 7.95
____	60570-4	Baby Talk	Lansky, B.	$ 4.95
____	54463-2	Best Baby Name Book, The	Lansky, B.	$ 3.95
____	54476-4	David, We're Pregnant!	Johnston, L.	$ 3.95
____	54477-2	Dear Babysitter	Lansky, V.	$ 7.95
____	54588-4	Dear Babysitter Refill Pad	Lansky, V.	$ 2.50
____	54464-0	Discipline Without Shouting or Spanking	Wyckoff/Unell	$ 4.95
____	54478-0	Do They Ever Grow Up?	Johnston, L.	$ 3.95
____	62278-1	Feed Me! I'm Yours	Lansky, V.	$ 6.95
____	54497-7	First Year Baby Care	Kelly, P.	$ 5.95
____	60569-0	Free Stuff for Kids	FSFK Editors	$ 3.50
____	54481-0	Grandma's Favorites Photo Album	Meadowbrook	$ 6.50
____	54482-9	Hi Mom! Hi Dad!	Johnston, L.	$ 3.95
____	62274-9	Mother Murphy's Law	Lansky, B.	$ 2.95
____	54543-4	My First Five Years Record Book	Meadowbrook	$10.95
____	54484-5	My First Year Calendar	Meadowbrook	$ 6.95
____	54485-3	My First Year Photo Album	Meadowbrook	$14.95
____	54486-1	Our Baby's First Year Calendar	Meadowbrook	$ 7.95
____	54487-X	Practical Parenting Tips	Lansky, V.	$ 6.95
____	54498-5	Pregnancy, Childbirth and the Newborn	Simkin/Whalley	$ 9.95
____	54467-5	Self-Esteem for Tots to Teens	Anderson, G.	$ 4.95
____	55611-8	Successful Breastfeeding	Dana/Price	$ 8.95
____	55692-4	10,000 Baby Names	Lansky, B.	$ 2.95
____	54495-0	You and Me Baby	Regnier, S.	$ 8.95

Please send me copies of the books checked above. I am enclosing $ _____ (full amount per each copy and $1.00 for first copy and $.50 for each additional copy to cover postage and handling. Order to be sent to Canada add $2.00 for extra postage. Overseas postage and handling will be billed). Quantity discounts on request. Allow up to four weeks for delivery.

Send check or money order to Meadowbrook, Inc. No cash or C.O.D.s, please.

Mail order to:
Book Orders
Meadowbrook, Inc.
18318 Minnetonka Blvd.
Deephaven, MN 55391

Phone orders: (612) 473-5400

For purchases over $10.00, you may use VISA or MasterCard (order by mail or phone). For these orders we need information below.

Charge to: ☐ VISA   ☐ MasterCard

Account # _____

Expiration Date _____

Card Signature _____

Send Book(s) to:

Name _____

Address _____

City _____ State _____ Zip _____